THE PHILLIP KEVEREN SERIES PIANO SOLO

16 ICONIC SONGS ARRANGED BY PHILLIP KEVEREN

ISBN 978-1-70516-132-6

Visit Hal Leonard Online at
www.halleonard.com

Visit Phillip at
www.phillipkeveren.com

World headquarters, contact:
Hal Leonard
7777 West Bluemound Road
Milwaukee, WI 53213
Email: info@halleonard.com

In Europe, contact:
Hal Leonard Europe Limited
42 Wigmore Street
Marylebone, London, W1U 2RY
Email: info@halleonardeurope.com

In Australia, contact:
Hal Leonard Australia Pty. Ltd.
4 Lentara Court
Cheltenham, Victoria, 3192 Australia
Email: info@halleonard.com.au

PREFACE

The songs of Stephen Sondheim are works of art that will charm, challenge, and inspire theatre audiences for many generations to come. These piano arrangements celebrate only half of Sondheim's brilliance – the music. His lyrics are truly astounding as well, with or without music.

A special thank you to Marek Norman, my composer friend of many decades, for his assistance in assembling the song list for this collection. Marek has mounted many Sondheim productions in his native Canada, and is a fount of information on his works. We have shared many a conversation on the whys and wherefores, twists and turns, of these magnificent songs.

As I often suggest to the pianist approaching a new arrangement, take the time to listen to a recording of the original song to get an overview of the composition. It will be a big help as you begin the process of learning the piano setting.

Sincerely,

Phillip Keveren

April 2022
Franklin, Tennessee

BIOGRAPHY

Phillip Keveren, a multi-talented keyboard artist and composer, writes original works in a variety of genres from piano solo to symphonic orchestra. He gives frequent concerts and workshops for teachers and their students in the United States, Canada, Europe, and Asia. Mr. Keveren holds a B.M. in composition from California State University Northridge and a M.M. in composition from the University of Southern California.

CONTENTS

ANYONE CAN WHISTLE

from ANYONE CAN WHISTLE

Words and Music by
STEPHEN SONDHEIM
Arranged by Phillip Keveren

21
p
25
cresc.
mf
29
33
mp
37
mf
p

41
mf
45
p
cresc.
f
49
53
mp
57
mf
p
molto rit.
3
3

CHILDREN WILL LISTEN

from INTO THE WOODS

Words and Music by
STEPHEN SONDHEIM
Arranged by Phillip Keveren

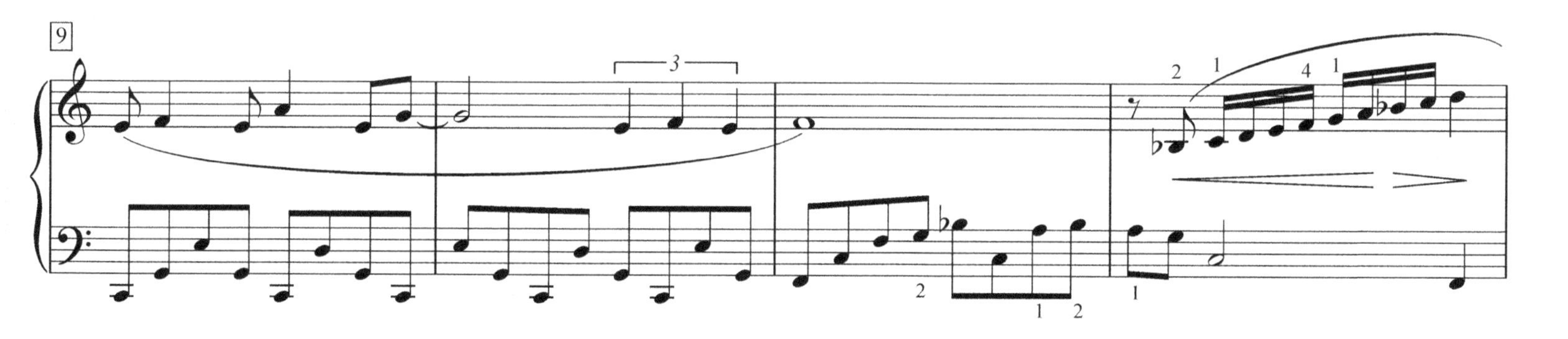

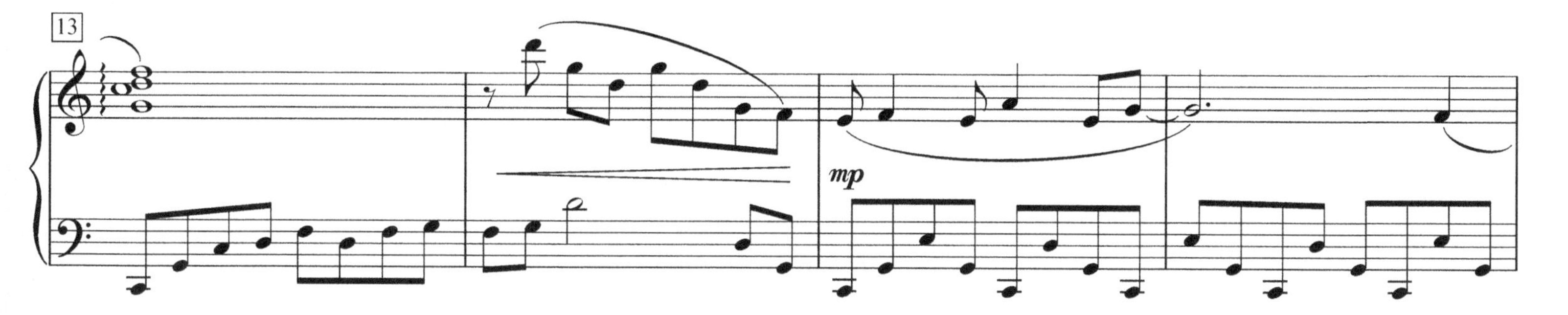

21
25
30
34
38
cresc. poco a poco

41
poco rit.
mf
a tempo
45
3
49
f
52
p
56
3
rit.
pp

BEING ALIVE
from COMPANY

Music and Lyrics by
STEPHEN SONDHEIM
Arranged by Phillip Keveren

16
19
cresc.
22
mf
p
cresc. poco a poco
25
28
f
8vb

31
34
37
40
43

46
50
53
p
cresc. poco a poco
57
8va
broaden
ff
8vb
60
(8va)

BROADWAY BABY
from FOLLIES

Music and Lyrics by
STEPHEN SONDHEIM
Arranged by Phillip Keveren

16
sfz
19
sim.
mp
22
25
f
mf
28
3
To Coda

31
34
37
40
43
f

46
49
52
D.S. al Coda
CODA
55
f
58
sffz

COMEDY TONIGHT

from A FUNNY THING HAPPENED ON THE WAY TO THE FORUM

Music and Lyrics by
STEPHEN SONDHEIM
Arranged by Phillip Keveren

25
f
30
mp
34
f
39
1.
44
2.
ff
sfz

GOOD THING GOING

from MERRILY WE ROLL ALONG

Music and Lyrics by
STEPHEN SONDHEIM
Arranged by Phillip Keveren

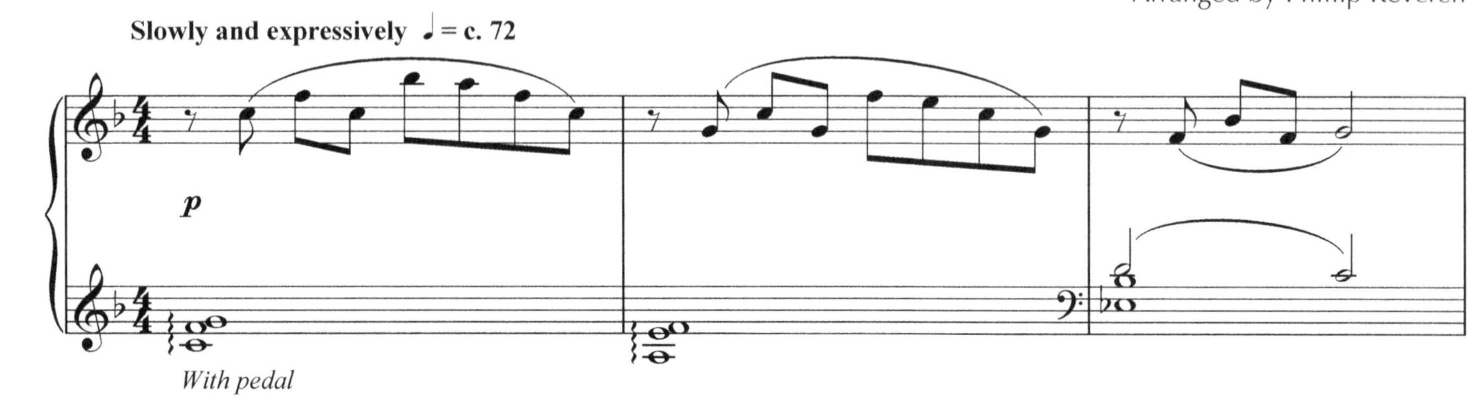

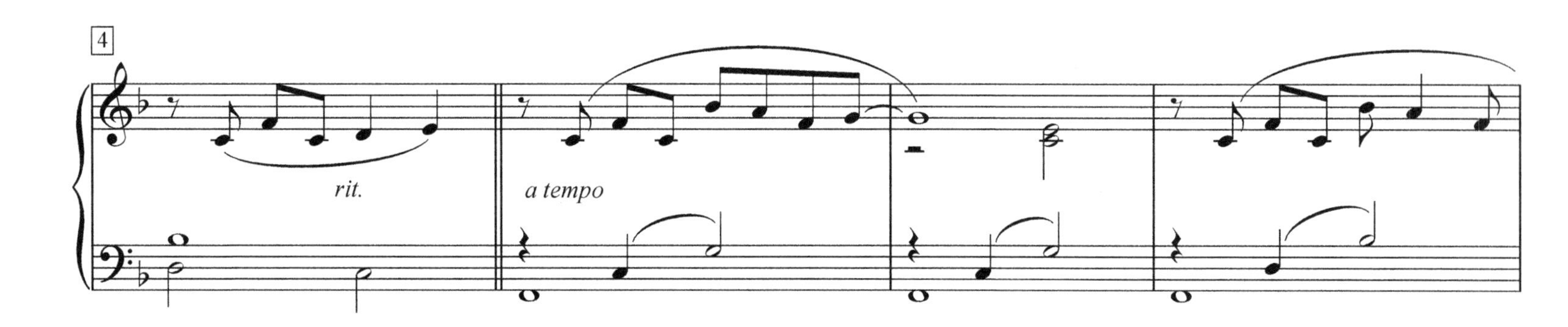

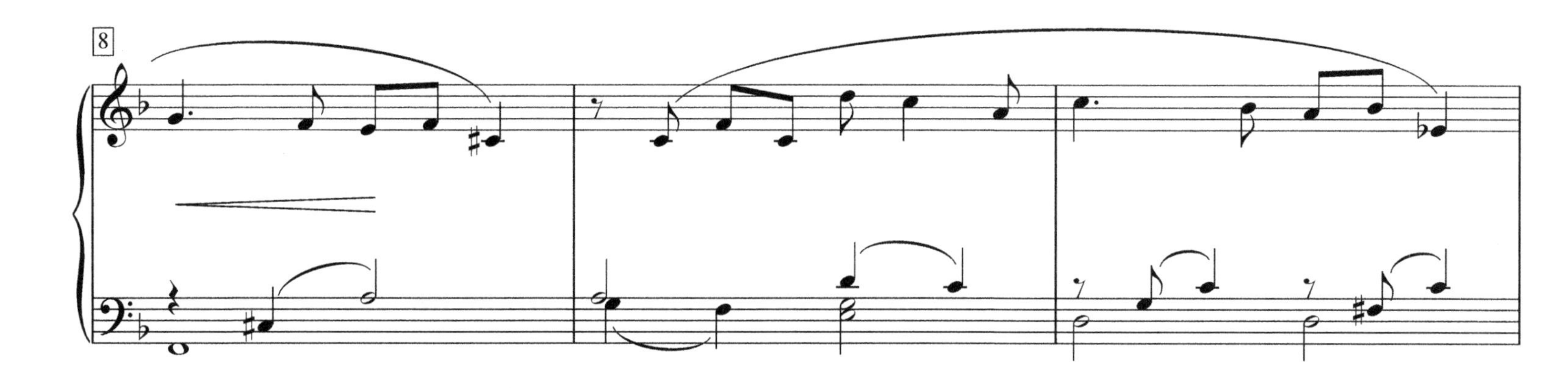

14
17
cresc.
mp
20
mf flowing
23
p cresc.
26
dim.
rit.

29
delicately
p a tempo
32
cresc.
35
mf
f
38
mf
mp
rit.
42
p
8vb

JOHANNA
from SWEENEY TODD

Music and Lyrics by
STEPHEN SONDHEIM
Arranged by Phillip Keveren

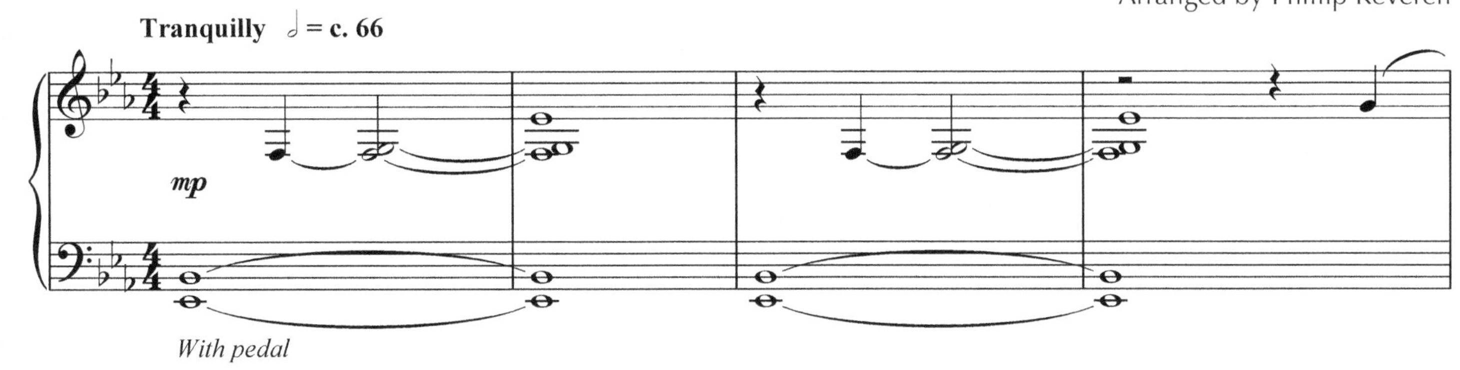

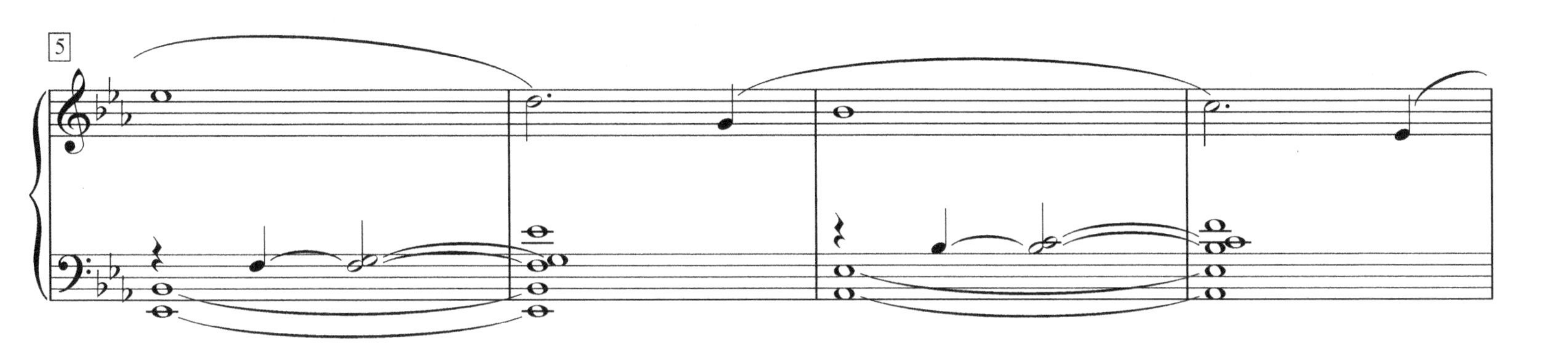

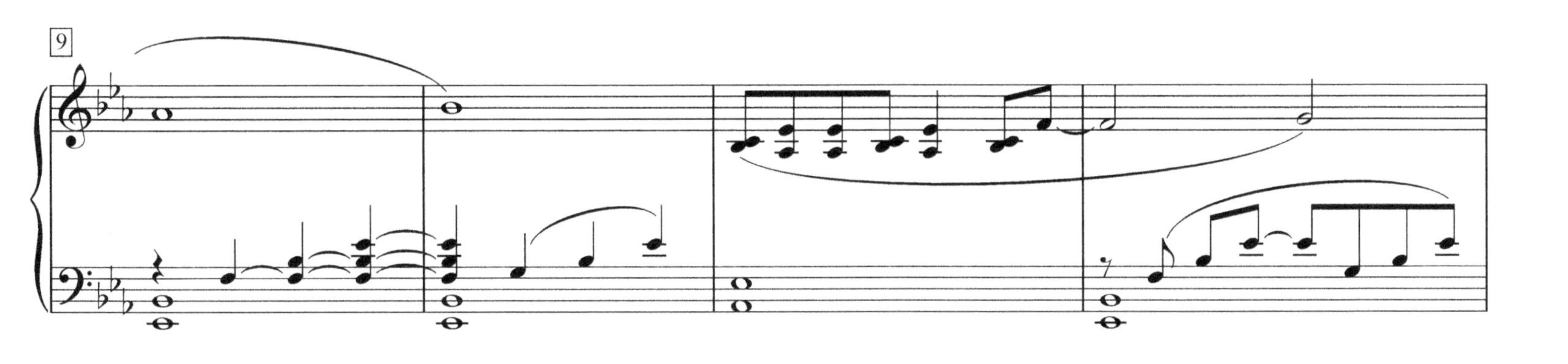

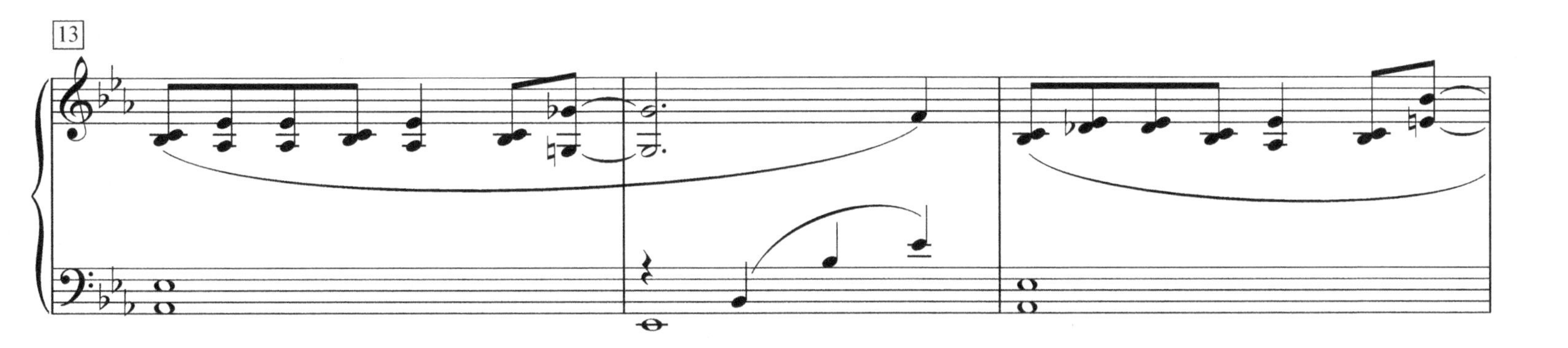

16
cresc. poco a poco
19
mf
23
mf
26
29
cresc.
f

33
Maestoso
38
dim.
43
mp
mf
47
f
50
L.H.
ff
L.H.

I REMEMBER

from the TV Production EVENING PRIMROSE

mp
p
pp
mp
pp
p
mf
rit.
pp
a tempo
f
p

36
cresc. poco a poco
3
f
3
40
p
43
pp
mp
45
pp
mp cresc.
47
f
rit. e dim.
6
1
1
1
1

50
mp a tempo
54
58
p
62
66
molto rit.

LOSING MY MIND
from FOLLIES

Words and Music by
STEPHEN SONDHEIM
Arranged by Phillip Keveren

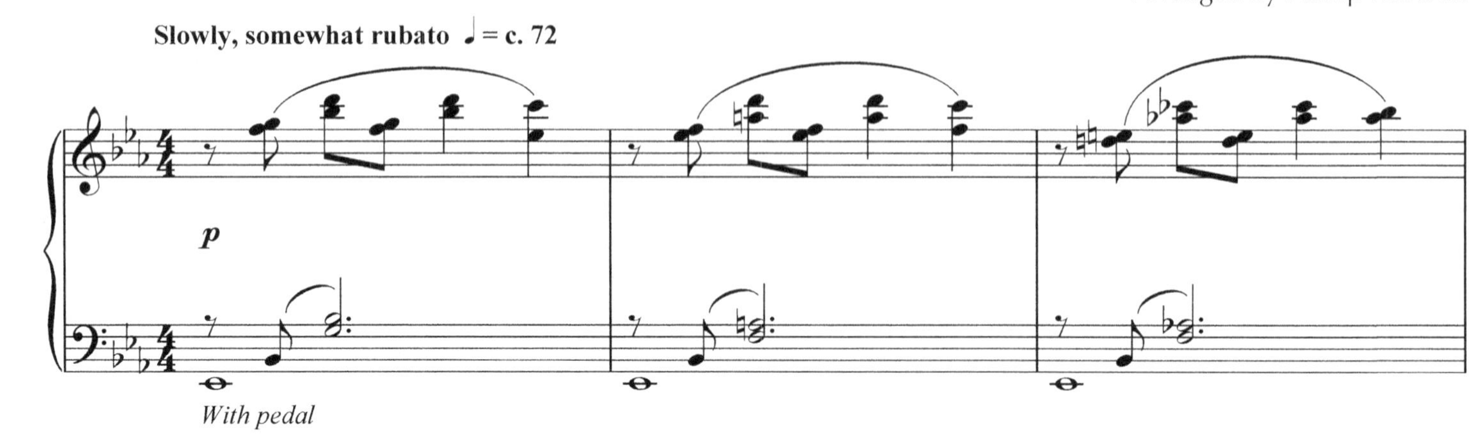

13
mp
16
19
mf
22
25

28
mp
31
rit.
34
ten.
a tempo
To Coda
37
mf
40
mp

43
46
49
mp
D.S. al Coda
52
CODA
54
pp

NO ONE IS ALONE
(Part 1)
from INTO THE WOODS

Words and Music by
STEPHEN SONDHEIM
Arranged by Phillip Keveren

17
p
mp
21
25
mf
1
1
29
mp
33
mf

37
p

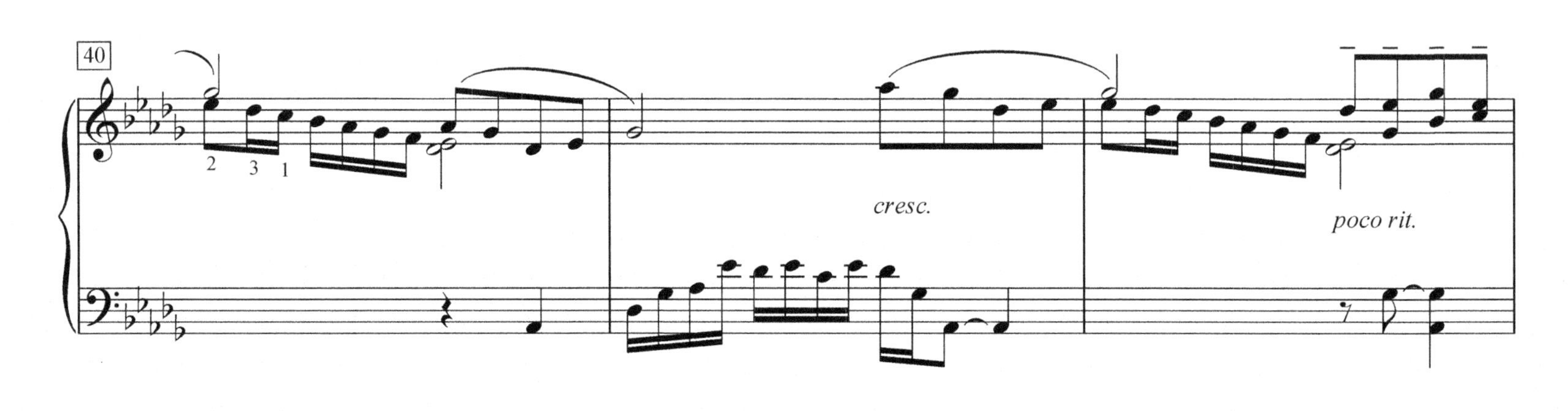
40
cresc.
poco rit.

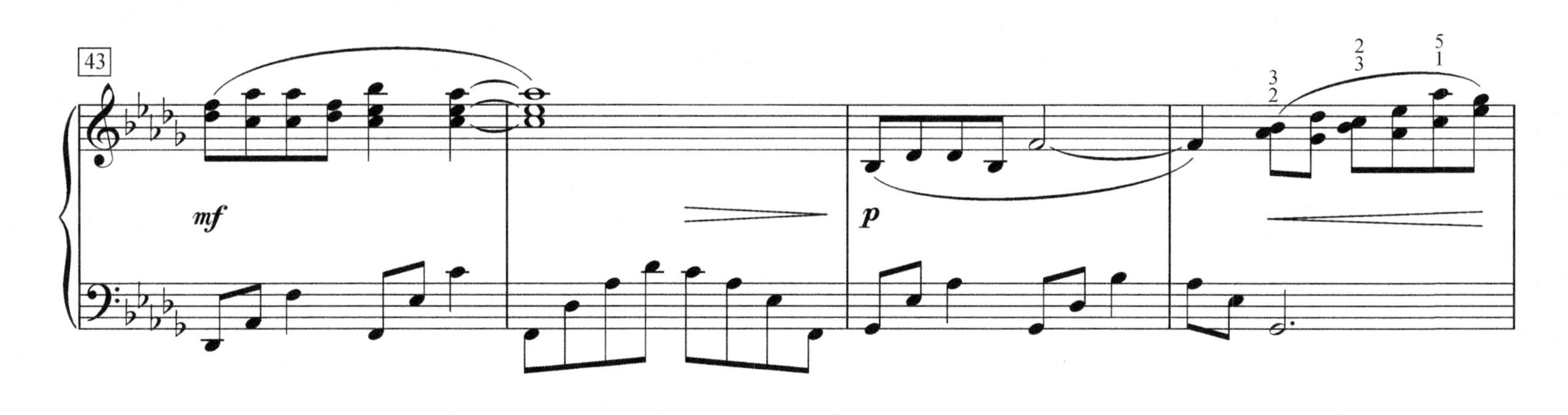
43
mf
p

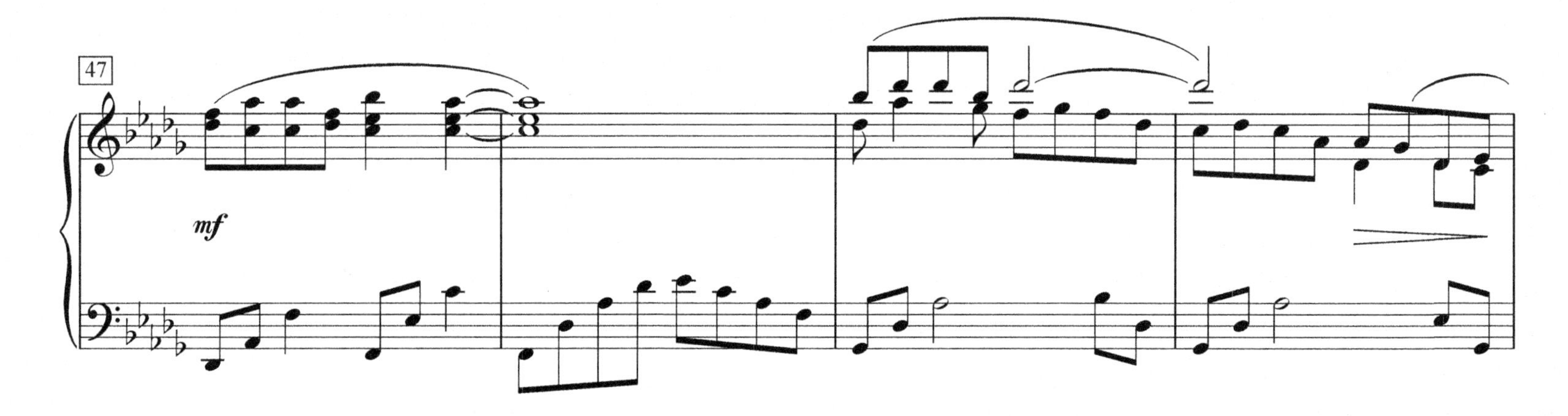
47
mf

51
dim. e rit.

Poco meno mosso
55
p

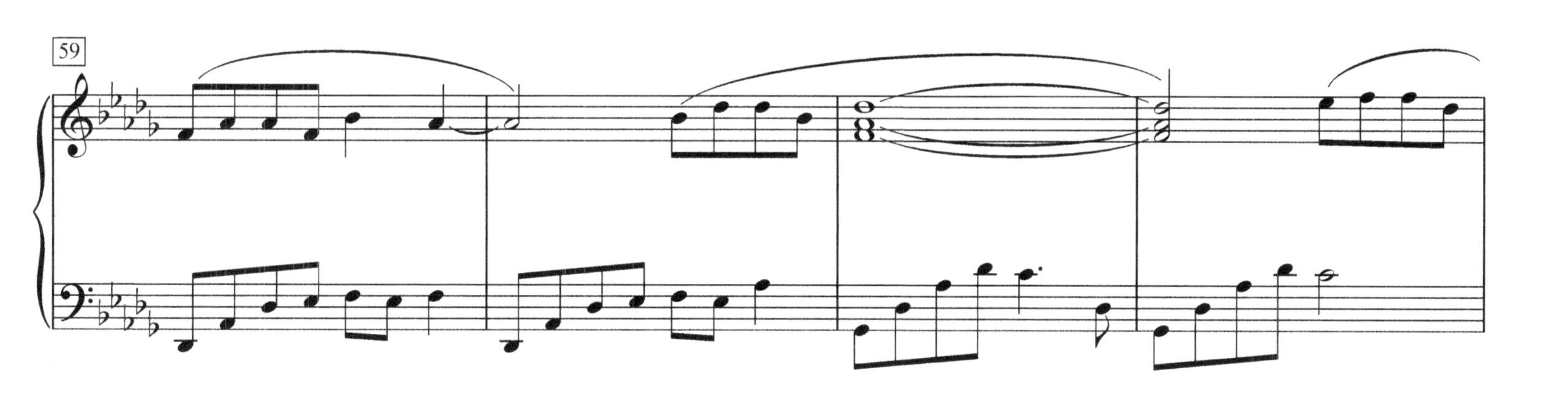
59

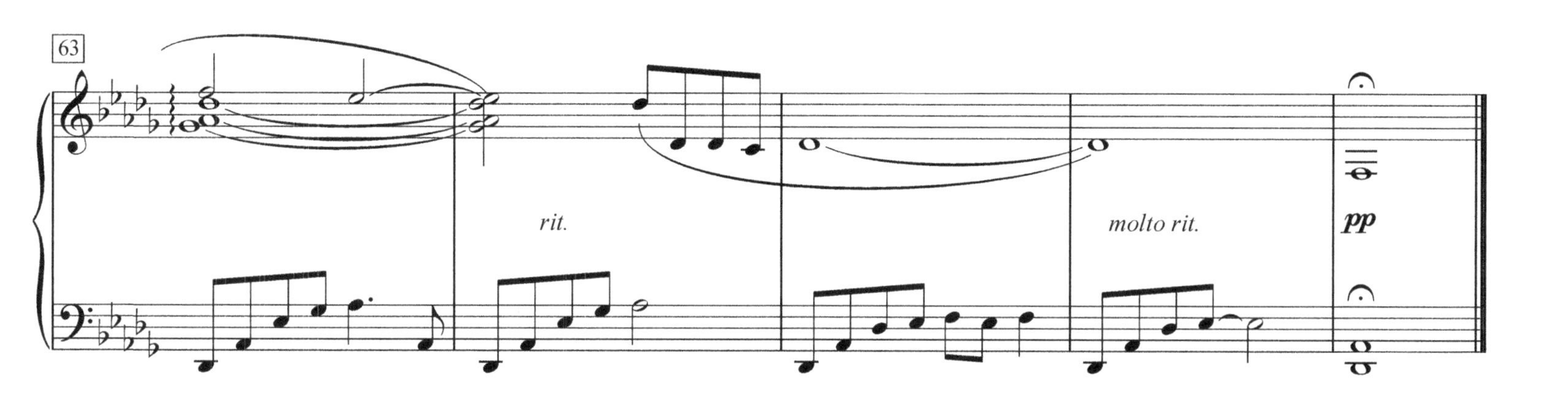
63
rit.
molto rit.
pp

NOT A DAY GOES BY

from MERRILY WE ROLL ALONG

Words and Music by
STEPHEN SONDHEIM
Arranged by Phillip Keveren

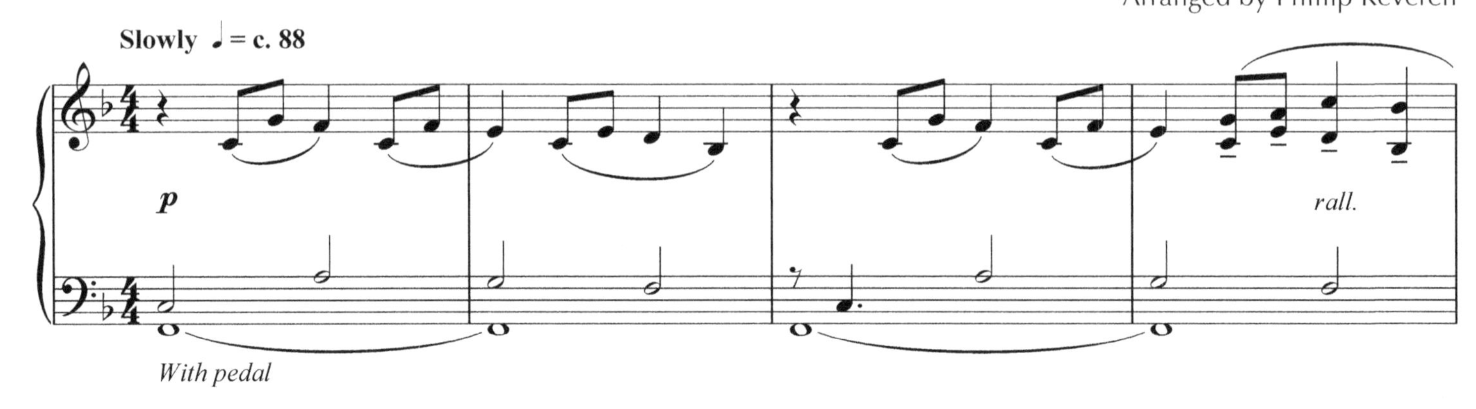

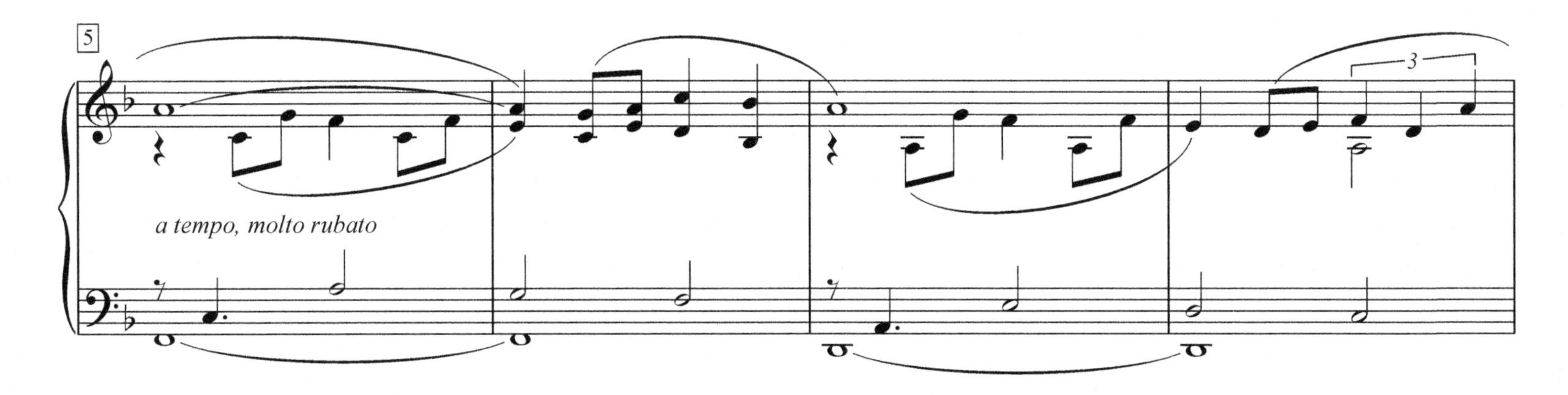

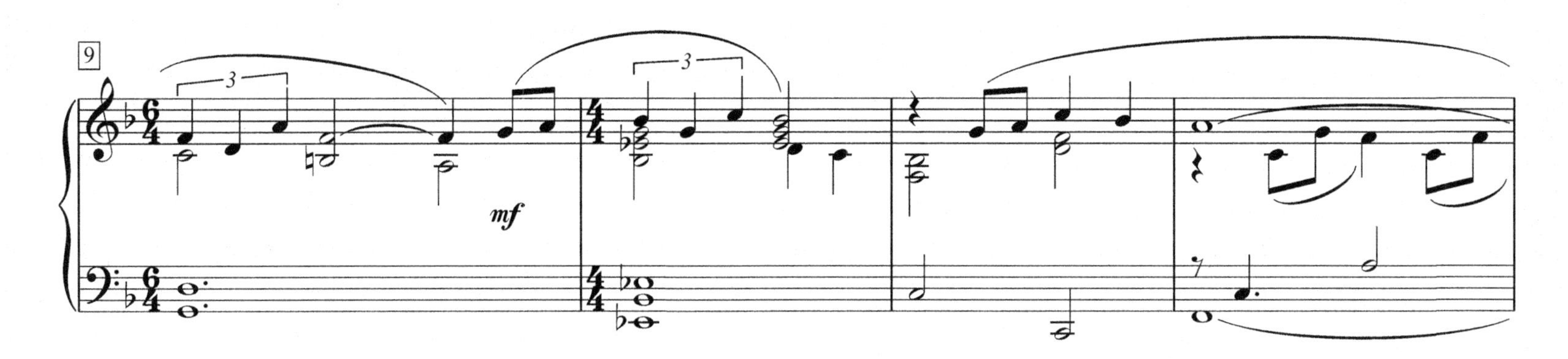

17
poco accel.
rit.
20
a tempo
poco cresc.
rit.
f a tempo
23
rall.
26
mf
29
cresc.
f
rit.

33
a tempo
p
36
cresc.
ff
39
42
mf
dim. poco a poco
45
p rit.
pp

NOT WHILE I'M AROUND

from SWEENEY TODD

Words and Music by
STEPHEN SONDHEIM
Arranged by Phillip Keveren

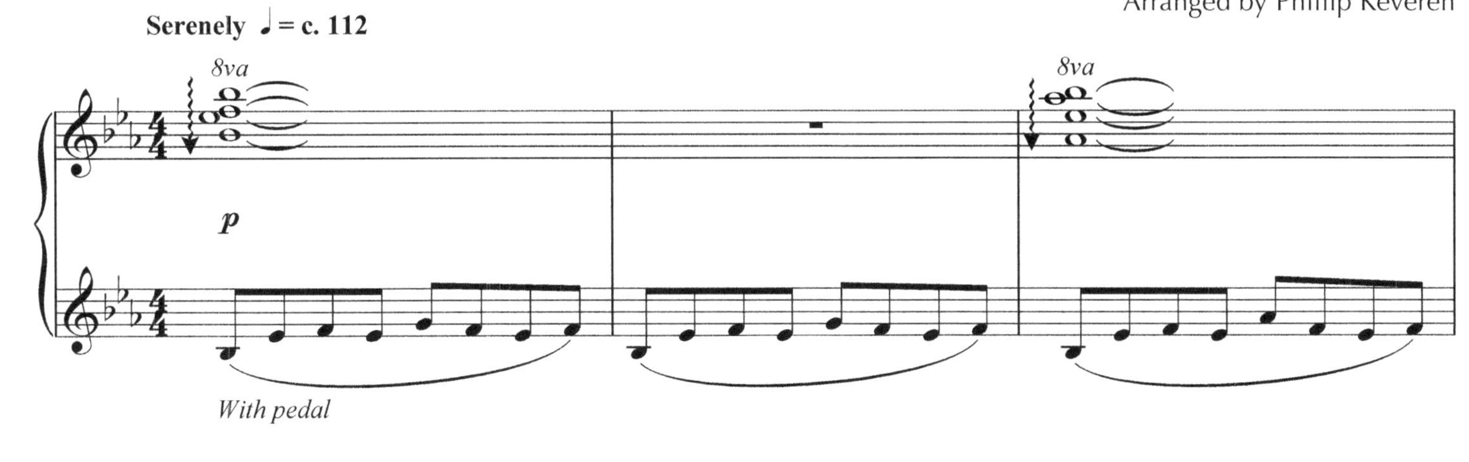

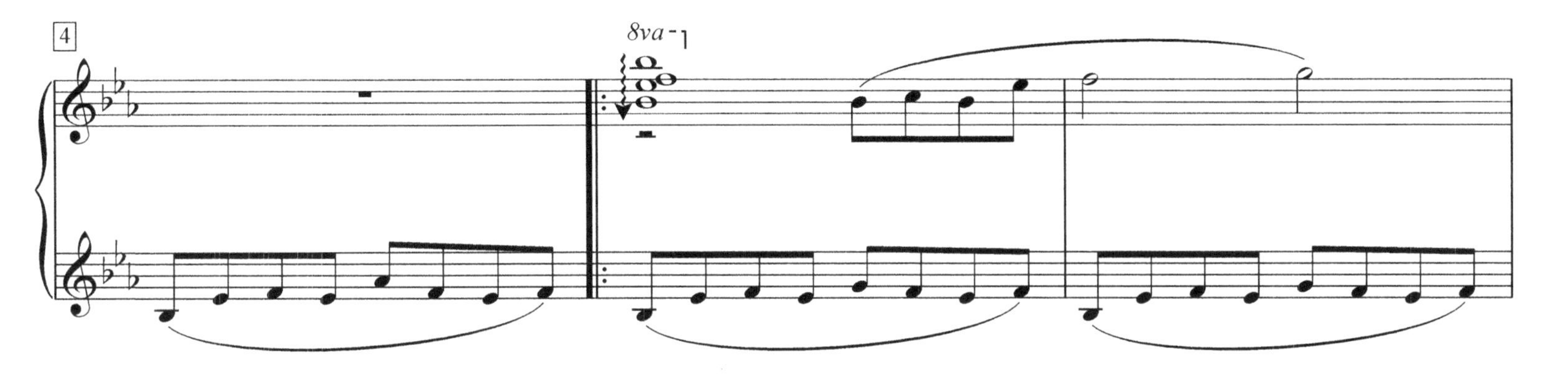

13
mf
dim.
16
rit.
mp a tempo
19
mf
molto rit.
dim.
22
mp a tempo

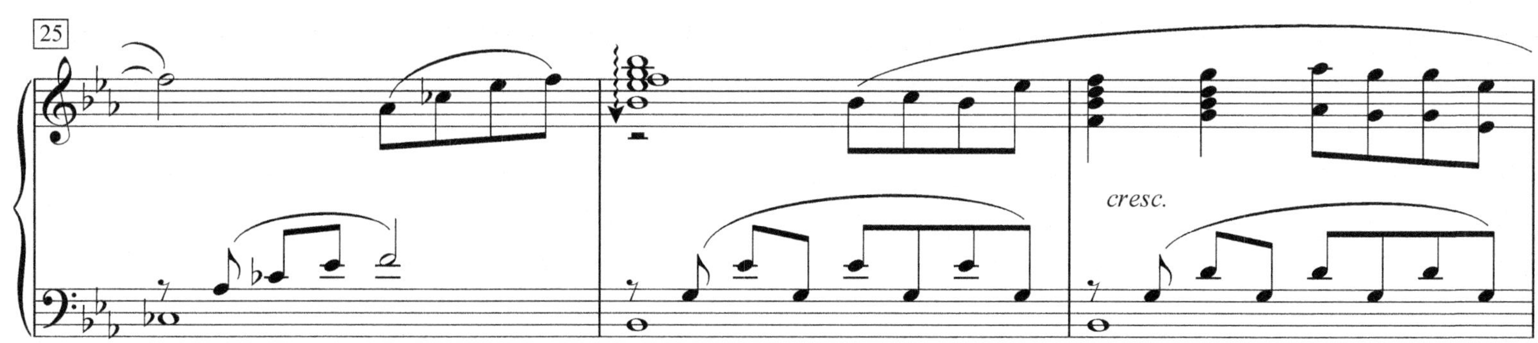
25
cresc.

28
f
31
rit. e dim.
1.
34
mp
p
a tempo
2.
38
mp
a tempo
42
8va
rit.
8va
R.H.
pp
8vb

OLD FRIENDS

from MERRILY WE ROLL ALONG

Words and Music by
STEPHEN SONDHEIM
Arranged by Phillip Keveren

23
cresc.
27
mf
rit. e dim.
pp
32
mp a tempo
p
37
cresc.
42
mf
47
mp cresc.
f

51
mp
55
cresc.
f
60
65
mf
70
f

75
80
84
89
molto rubato
95
sfz

PRETTY WOMEN

from SWEENEY TODD

Words and Music by
STEPHEN SONDHEIM
Arranged by Phillip Keveren

25
f
dim.
mf
30
mp
cresc. poco a poco
35
8va
mf
mf
p cresc.
39
f
43
8va
rit. e dim.
p
pp

SEND IN THE CLOWNS

from A LITTLE NIGHT MUSIC

Words and Music by
STEPHEN SONDHEIM
Arranged by Phillip Keveren

10
13
15
mp

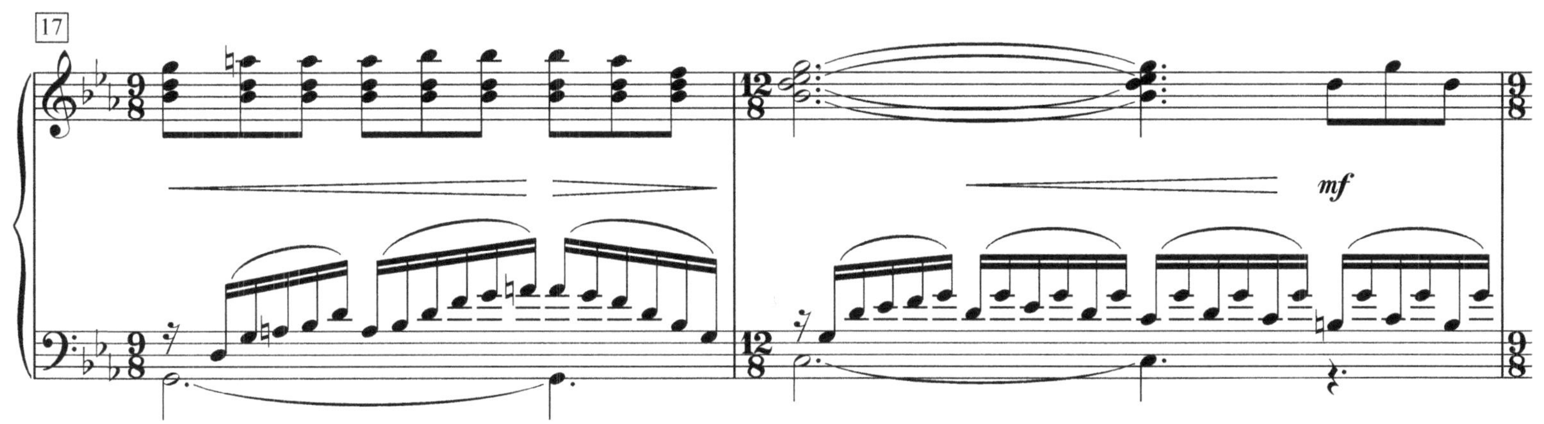
17
mf

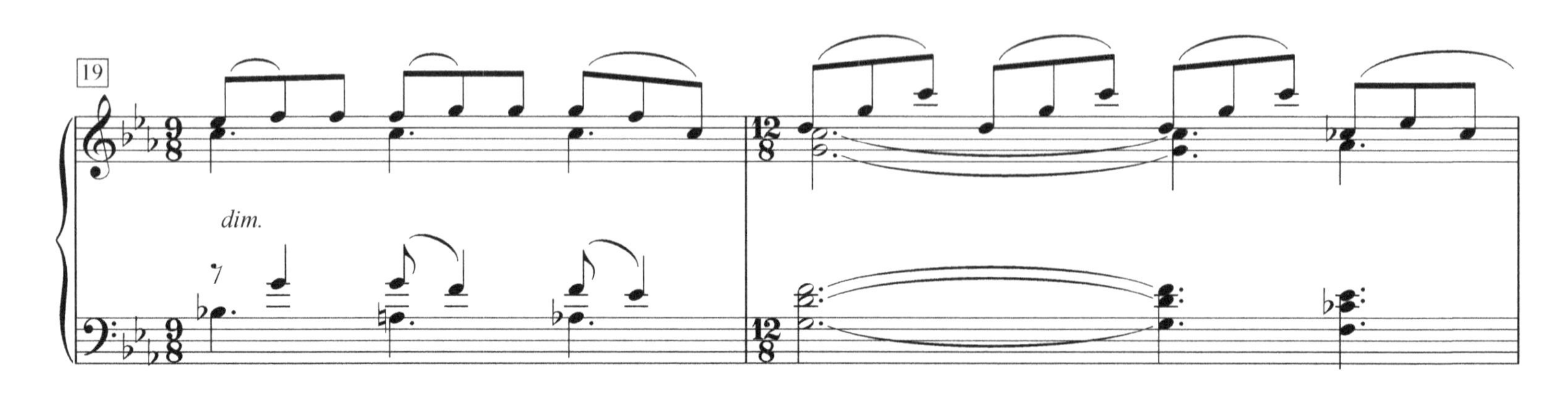
19
dim.

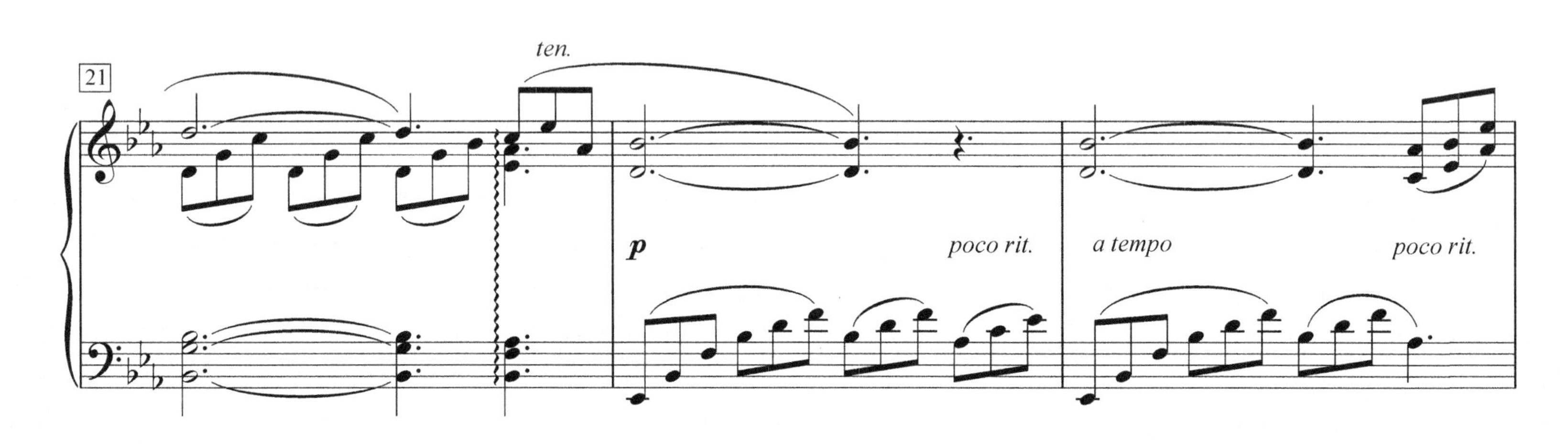
21
ten.
p
poco rit.
a tempo
poco rit.

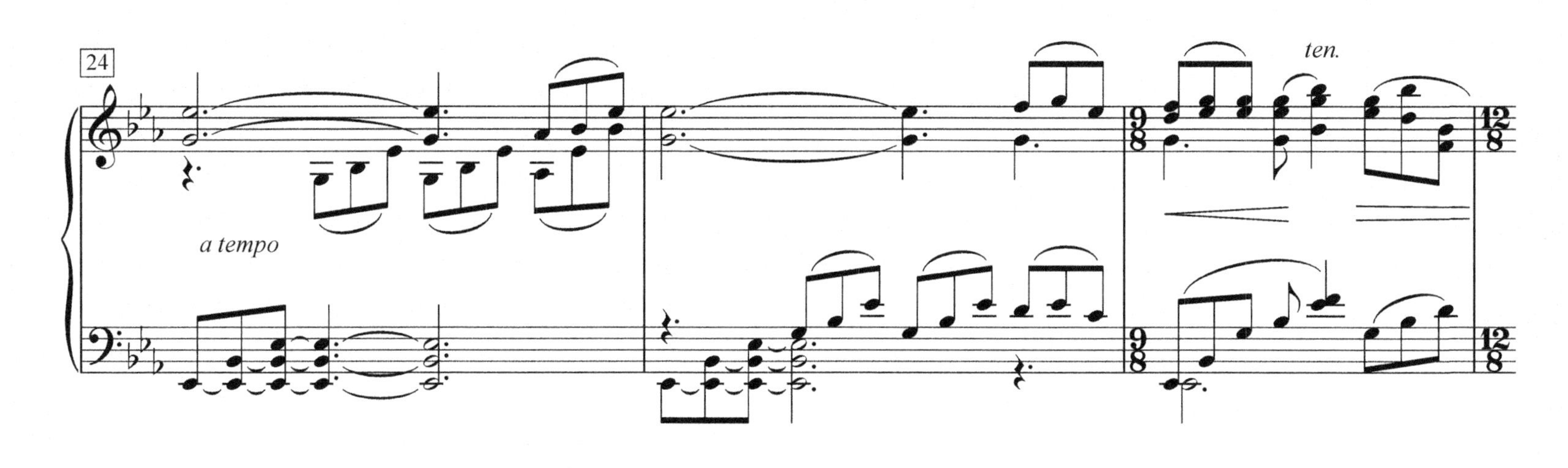
24
ten.
a tempo

27

30
cresc.
poco rit.
32
mf a tempo
34
ten.
rit.
mp
hesitantly
a tempo
37
p
rit.
a tempo
ten.
rit.
8va
pp

SUNDAY

from SUNDAY IN THE PARK WITH GEORGE

Words and Music by
STEPHEN SONDHEIM
Arranged by Phillip Keveren

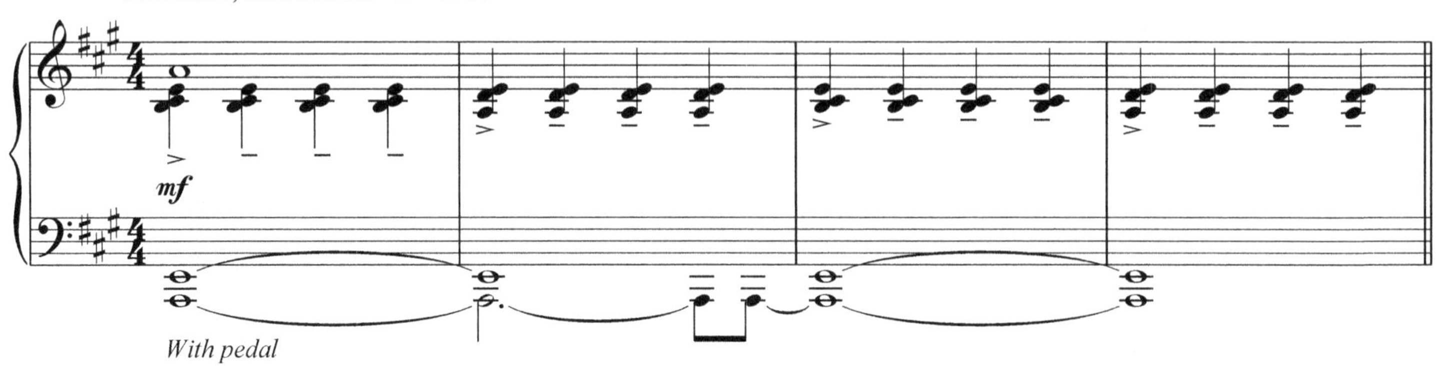

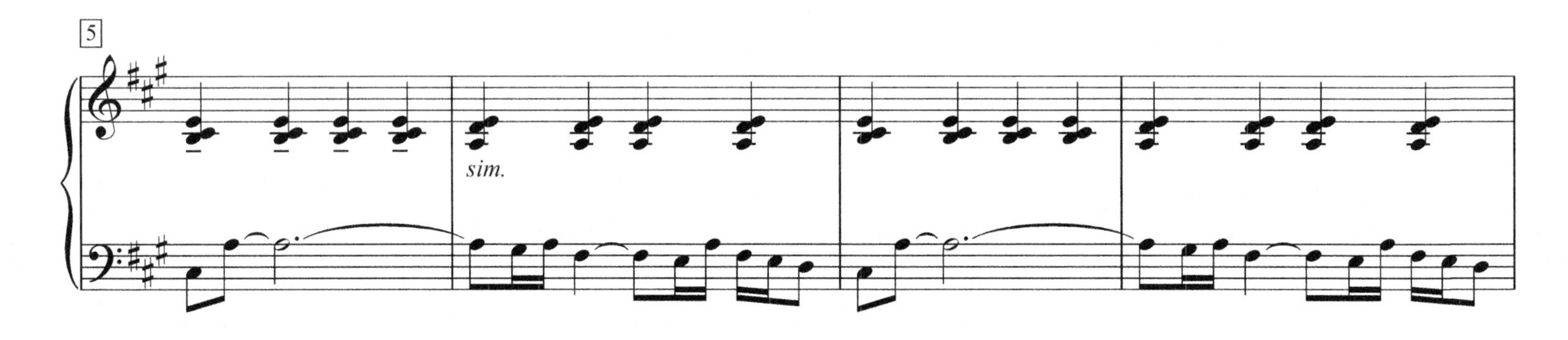

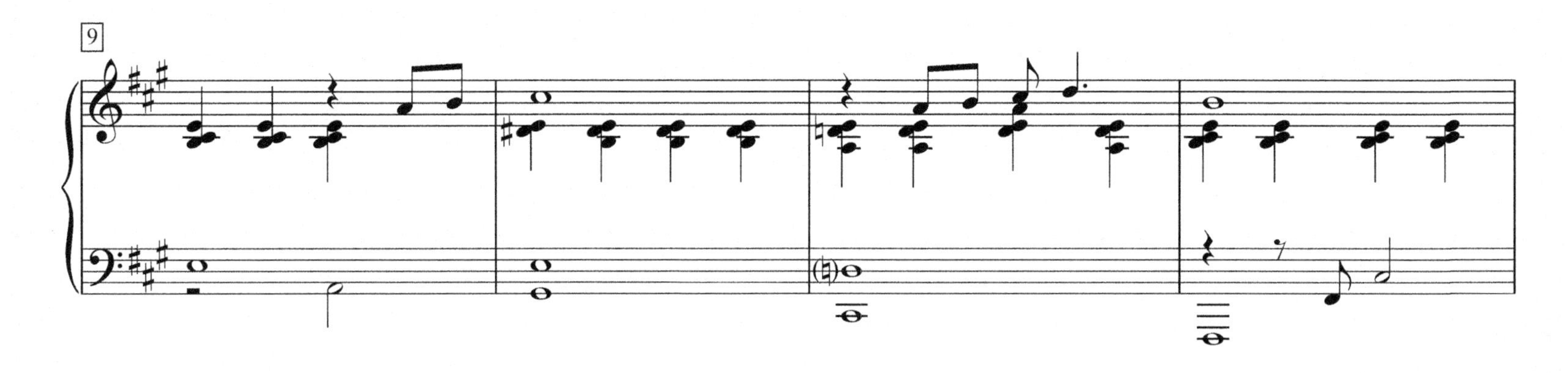

17
f
21
dim.
molto cresc.
poco rit.
25
f a tempo
28
dim.
32
mp
(L.H.)

36
40
44
f
cresc. poco a poco
rall.
48
ff a tempo
(R.H.)
51
(R.H.)
ten.
ten.